FEELINGS
YOU ALWAYS HAD BUT NEVER DARED TO NAME

Wendy Danforth • Illustrated by Artemus Cole

Health Communications, Inc. • Deerfield Beach, Florida

© 1992 Wendy Danforth and Artemus Cole
ISBN 1-55874-230-1

Publisher: Health Communications, Inc.
3201 S.W. 15th Street
Deerfield Beach, Florida 33442-8190

Dedication

To all of my dogs:
the ones who've gone,
the ones with me now and
the ones who will one day come
along, but most of all,
to my Harry.

Acknowledgement

My gratitude goes to Marie Stilkind who noodled me
until this book was done, to Nichole, Elizabeth and Ray Hess
for their cheering section, to Dr. Marvin Babyatsky who kept
my head attached to my neck, and to Father Ted Holt for
his inspiration and bringing me home.

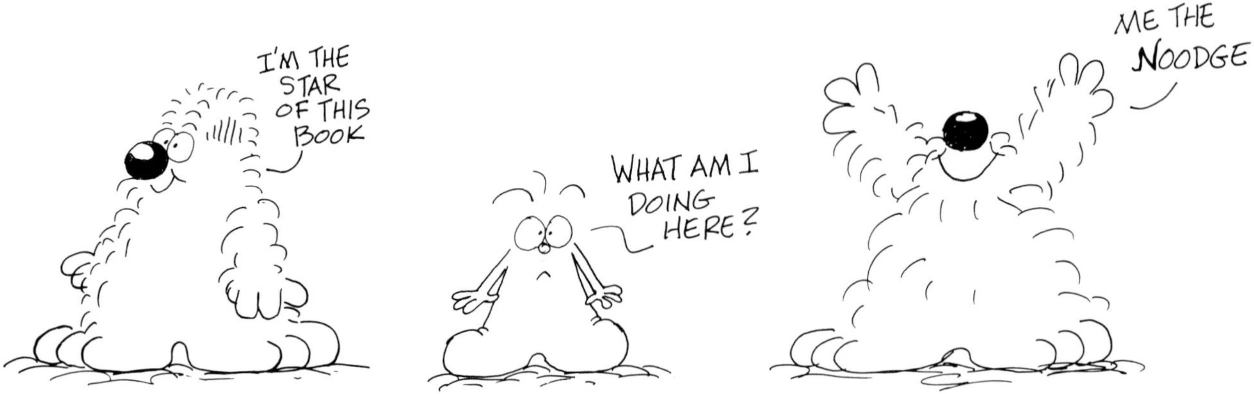
I'M THE STAR OF THIS BOOK
WHAT AM I DOING HERE?
ME THE NOODGE

INTRODUCTION

Inside each of us, there's a vulnerable part that
sometimes feels bewildered and a knowledgeable part that
can put life more into perspective. The NIP and the NOODGE will
make you laugh and stop fretting about all those feelings
you've always had but never dared to name.

The two characters here are basically the same "person"
inside all of us. Our Feeling, Nip, and our
Comforter, Noodge, sort of . . . .

KLUNKS:

A Klunk is a sad, heavy feeling that settles around your heart, viscera, tummy when you have experienced a loss . . . or you fear you have lost something such as when you have a fight with your friend, mate or anyone you love. Klunks feel like they'll never go away (the day your dog died).

NOODGE:

Klunks go away after enough time has passed.
The bigger the Klunk, the longer it takes.
But be assured — it will go away.

HOWMAGONNAS:

... The feeling of "How am I going to do it?" No one ever jumps off the bus the way Julie Andrews did in *The Sound Of Music,* singing "I have *confidence* in me!" And if you think you are the only one with the Howmagonnas, think again. Everyone wonders how in the world they're going to do whatever they set out to do, and some even wonder how on earth they ever did it when they succeed. There's another group that worries when "they" will find out that it was all a hoax even when they did it and it was successful.

NOODGE:

How are you going to do it?
One step at a time — the best way you can. It
helps to know that everyone feels the same way. How
do you suppose underarm deodorant got so popular?

FOBOS:

Feelings of abandonment or fright . . . a bunch of FoBos will give you at least one, but probably many phobias. The fear of feeling that abandoned feeling will cause you to freeze *all* your feelings. In all cases, FoBos stem from childhood when you were afraid that your parents might leave you forever (die), forget to collect you from wherever they had left you, send you to camp when you were too young to tie your own shoelaces . . . or withdraw love if you were bad.

NOODGE:

You're okay now. You survived and now *you* have control of your life. If someone you love abandons you, you'll survive it . . . they weren't right for you anyway. Step away from those crutches that everyone encourages you to use . . . like blaming everything on your childhood.

GLEEWEES:

Excited feelings that waft through you like tiny waves . . . gleeful feelings that produce the verbal: *"Wheee!"*

NOODGE:

Too many people think being blase is sophisticated. It's really boring. If you get Gleewees, don't let anyone snicker them away and when you find others who get Gleewees . . . hang on to them.

WAPPERS!

Feelings that raise the hairs on your neck, shivers down the spine.
They can range from fear to ecstasy . . . and many times happen
when you've created something, let it get cold and returned to it.
Hairs raising on the neck are reliable feeling indicators
because they can't be controlled.

NOODGE:

Do not permit anyone to discourage your feelings. No matter how "expert" the discouraging . . . follow your own feelings. In this case they come from the universal consciousness of Absolute Truth.

AND IN 1978 I SHOULDA SAID...

GREAVALS:

Feelings of unresolved grief, large
or small . . . they sometimes show up
in the form of a nodule in your muscle
when you're getting a massage.
Greavals are because of so much
stuff you never dared to say to
someone who is/was in control
of your life . . . anger you
never dared to express . . .
which, of course, produces
a certain kind
of unresolved
grief inside.

NOODGE:

Try this. Take as many paper cups as you need . . . one for each grief, each hurt, each anger you still feel. Label the bottom of the cups . . . turn them upside down, then stamp on them one at a time. As they pop, stamp the next. Stamp/pop/stamp/pop. Shout, "Yeah!" each time one pops and shout again, "You're gone!"

After each cup has been stamped out, give yourself a hug. Any time those feelings resurface, picture the popped cup and shout, "You're gone! Stamped out!" . . . and start being kinder to yourself. You don't need that footprint on your back any longer.

KAFLOOEYS:

A person you love snaps at you . . . the sun doesn't shine . . . someone else is center stage. These are feelings you can't explain. It's the sunny side of yuck. You don't feel ill, you just sort of feel Kaflooey. Sometimes, Kaflooeys come upon you suddenly, like when you feel someone isn't listening to you or you don't make a big hit at the new group's party. It gnaws at you, making you feel like the new kid in school.

NOODGE:

Go ahead and admit it when you feel
Kaflooey. Everyone likes a person
who is unafraid to admit they
feel insecure. It makes *them*
feel less insecure.

ARONO:

(aka IOWENO) These feelings come over you when you don't know
the answer to something . . . and rather than admit
you don't know, you lie.

NOODGE:

No one knows the answer to everything. Did you ever hear of any human who did?

NEGS:

Feelings that are always negative. Those with these feelings
are also called Negs. Think of any negative in the world about
any positive action, thought, dream or accomplishment
and the Negs will be throwing off Negs.

NOODGE:

Yuck. Get away from these feelings and these people!

WIGGLE WERPS:

Restless, irritable feelings that make you snap at someone, have restless legs. You can't sit still, get annoyed by things that normally don't bother you, feel impatient, itch. Your ticks come out (everyone has them) and you don't know what to do with your hands.

NOODGE:

Your best bet here is to get off by yourself and try to figure out what on earth is hassling you. It may be something as simple as the barometric pressure . . . or maybe you need more laughter and need to rent a funny movie. The main thing is you MUST find out just what the burr under your saddle is. These feelings are subconscious door-bangers. You've ignored some deep need and your Self is now trying to get your attention by making sure you can't ignore your needs any longer.

MALOOOOOOOS:

Feelings that begin in your solar plexus and travel, without control, to your vocal chords . . . producing a howl-like sound. These feelings may be joyous or very deeply sad. Wolves howl . . . it's the same thing. Early Native Americans did it freely.

NOODGE:

If you feel inhibited about your Maloooos, get over it. Let them happen. In all cases, Maloooos are healing. The shower is a great place to have Maloooos . . . or alone in your car.

ERRUMS:

The feeling that you want
to apologize . . . make things
right because you know you
are wrong. You have wrongly
accused or misjudged and hurt
someone but you have now waited
too long, making it worse by this
waiting because of your pride.

NOODGE:

So what *is* your priority in this case? Your pride or your relationship? Would you rather be right or would you rather be happy?

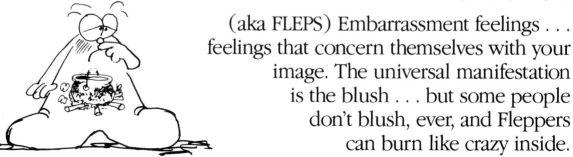

FLEPPERS:

(aka FLEPS) Embarrassment feelings . . .
feelings that concern themselves with your
image. The universal manifestation
is the blush . . . but some people
don't blush, ever, and Fleppers
can burn like crazy inside.

NOODGE:

Very uncomfortable . . . but gee whiz, it happens. You can't do anything about it *except* try to laugh at yourself and not dwell on the event for days and days. Some people anguish over it for decades. . . . If you permit this, you're self-destructing.

AWWWWWS:

An overwhelming and sudden feeling of being touched, seeing something adorable . . . wonderful. Awwwws are enhanced by verbalization and even more so in group verbalization.

NOODGE:

Awwwww!

TILTS:

You had Tilts when you were a kid and you still have them. Tilts are feelings when your parents/grown-up-in-charge . . . mate/boss/ pal . . . "loses it" . . . yells, gets irrationally angry. Your feelings glaze, cloud . . . you're plum scared. You want to be invisible. Your world tilts . . .. It's a bad dream. You feel off-kilter . . . *tilted.* What was it *you did* to make this happen?

NOODGE:

NOTHING. Grown-ups, people-in-charge, mates, bosses, all have the same feelings, fears, insecurities you have. They handle some well, some not so well and no one handles everything well all the time. When they caused a Tilt in you, they were probably scared . . . rejected, felt they had lost an image . . .
Anger is fear with a chin jutted out.

LESSEES:

These feelings are the ones that make you unable to listen when someone else is speaking to you because you are always saying to yourself, "Lessee . . . when can I safely interrupt and get my point in?" You aren't listening to the other person because you are structuring and restructuring your own point (which, by the way, may have passed its appropriateness long ago). These feelings also have you asking yourself, while you are talking, "Lessee . . . I wonder how I look . . ." or "I wonder who is agreeing with me . . ." People with an abundance of Lessee feelings can't resist peering at themselves in every mirror they pass.

NOODGE:

Well, who's the loser here?
Talking to you has got to
be like talking to a wall.

SANDBAGGED:

The feeling of anger, amazement, disbelief that you've been Sand-bagged . . . someone took advantage of you . . . you did something you didn't want to do . . . you never got that loan repaid . . . you paid too much for something . . . you found out you'd been lied to . . . or you were dumped by your company or your relationship.

NOODGE:

These feelings can cause a real dip in your self-esteem, but PULEEZE don't go blaming it on your childhood and don't say you'll never trust anyone again . . . just be more aware. And stomping on some upturned paper cups wouldn't hurt right now.

WILLOWIUMS:

Feelings similar to the behavior of a willow tree . . . blowing this way and that way with the wind. A need-to-sit-on-the-fence feeling, for fear of not being permitted to stay safely in the herd. This feeling permits no stance, opinion or set of values of your own.

HEY, GUYS— WHATEVER YOU WANT TO DO I WANT TO DO TOO!

NOODGE:

Sheep behave this way. You are not a
sheep. You do not need to be
in a herd . . . Do ewe?

Baaaaa-a-a-aa!

WHIZZLES:

Whizzles are feelings that *feel like* butterflies in your tummy . . . but this Whizzle thing goes a little deeper. Whizzles whiz around in your viscera, through your heartstrings and into your brain. It's a feeling of anticipation mingled with fright . . . an "Oh gosh, I hope I don't mess up" feeling. You also get Whizzles when you feel trapped.

NOODGE:

It's okay to have these feelings as long as they don't block you from doing anything because you fear them. You have control . . . it's okay to have the feeling, *any* feeling. You can share them, wear them, repair them and live through them, with them and in spite of them.

DAAWS:

The feeling that came over you
when you missed the point, didn't get the joke . . .
or when you hadn't been listening and you asked a question
that had obviously already been answered and everyone knew it.

NOODGE:

Laugh at yourself and admit you don't get it . . . or that your mind had wandered and say you're sorry. Since this happens to absolutely everyone, you'll be forgiven.

FIGGERS:

These are "that figures . . ." feelings . . . a why-me?/why-not-me? feeling. These feelings cause you to always be figuring people out . . . figuring what their angle is . . . what's the catch? What's in it for me?

NOODGE:

Go figure how you can
get more out of your life
without so much figgering.

WUMMERS:

A rush-like, warm, yummy feeling that sort of hums through you . . . .
Wummmmmm. Someone says something wonderful to you or
about you. Some people get Wummers when they take
that first bite of a hot-fudge sundae.

NOODGE:

Yum, yum, wummmmmm.

KAHZIPS:

Feelings of being rushed
all the time . . . huff-puff,
huff-puff. The White
Rabbit in Lewis Carroll's
Alice In Wonderland had
Kahzips *all* the time. If you
are prone to having Kahzips,
you are probably late
to everything.

NOODGE:

Set your clocks three hours ahead, then when you think you're out of time, you'll enjoy at least three hours a day of your life. (Moreover, you'll stop being late to everything, which is telling everyone, by this behavior, that your time is more valuable than theirs.) Always on-the-go precludes really enjoying that proverbial moment. Try to stop feeling guilty for relaxing and doing something just-for-the-fun-of-it.

S'OVERS:

The feeling that "it's all over" . . . whatever or whoever it involves.
A lackluster feeling that prompts you to ask yourself,
"What do I need with this?"

NOODGE:

Really? Or is it that commitment is just too inconvenient for you?

DINKY DEWS:

Feelings of being all choked up. A tear is longing to be permitted to fall. Dinkey Dews are also caused by unshared dreams . . . untried goals, long ago sadness that went unsoothed and got held back. Dinkey Dews cause you to live a life of always holding back in an effort to save yourself the hurt or rejection that causes the Dinkey Dews.

NOODGE:

Have a good, long Maloooo . . . go ahead
and say, "Ain't it awful?" . . . own the
hurt or rejection, let the tear fall . . .
then move on.

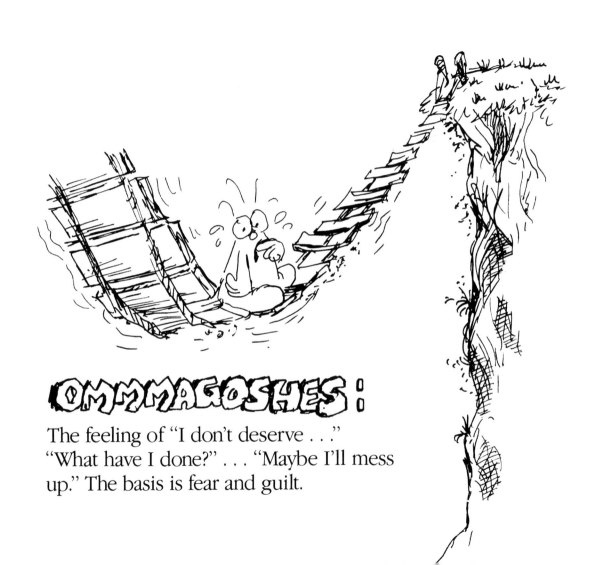

OMMMAGOSHES:

The feeling of "I don't deserve . . ."
"What have I done?" . . . "Maybe I'll mess
up." The basis is fear and guilt.

NOODGE:

Get out of the rain. Why
do you stay under that personal
little cloud of gloom and doom?
Maybe you didn't "do" anything . . .
and maybe you *will* mess up. But
you're human, aren't you?
Admit it and be gentle
to yourself and others.

THE PURPLE FEELING:

Everyone has one and only one Purple Feeling. It gets all puffed up
when you feel wonderful or proud, loving, validated, secure and safe.
When you feel threatened or too much is being asked of you or
you don't want to get involved, the Purple Feeling shrinks up into
a teeny, tiny dot.

NOODGE:

Once your Purple Feeling becomes a dot,
it may take some time for it to repuff
(refill). A pat on the head helps or
a "Hey, that's okay." Absolutely
everyone has this same feeling
. . . it just takes different
buttons to push it up
and down.

FOOLERS:

Feelings that you are fooling everyone. Someone you love, loves
you . . . so either something is wrong with that
person (because you know in your heart you
don't deserve to be loved) *or* you must be
fooling them. So you go on, secretly aware that
you are only fooling . . . waiting for the day
when they discover the real you and
stop loving you.

NOODGE:

There are many selves inside of you, changing at the drop of a hat depending on the circumstances. If you admit this to yourself and those around you, you will have stopped "fooling" and once you see that it's okay to be all those selves, you won't feel scared that the real you is unworthy of love. It'll save you a whole *bunch* of time and worry.

BIDDLES:

Feeling of being small . . . (as in "Iddle-Biddle") unable to
"measure up." *Everyone* carries these feelings around . . .
probably because deep down inside we're all kids . . .
and a little scared. If you are functioning in work,
play, relationships, sex, life, you are working
through your Biddles.

NOODGE:

If you claim that you never have the Biddles, you are suffering from delusions of grandeur.

OOGA BOOGAS:

Feelings that make you want to cry . . . generally bring on a
stuffed nose . . . wheezing. These feelings may even give you
allergies. You are stuffed up, blocked, choked because you dare
not say what's on your mind or even admit that you are feeling
threatened or afraid. These feelings come over you when
you remember something from a long time ago.

NOODGE:

What are you afraid will happen if you let go of whatever or whomever you are holding on to? Give yourself permission to be in charge of your own life. Gradually drift away from the friend who continually makes you feel uncertain about yourself . . . or confront that person to give the friendship a chance to change. Start looking for another job if the one you're in makes you feel imprisoned. You have a right to be happy and the right to make this happen.

SNUGAMORES:

(Italian, originally pronounced Snug-a-mooray) These snuggling feelings happen when you snuggle, fall into a clean, puffy warm bed, feel secure, love and are loved in return or just get a pat on the head. . . . Old movies do this to you sometimes . . . happy endings . . . hot soup . . . a breeze, warm sun on your face. Snugamores come upon you when you know you don't have to go anywhere or say anything for a whole evening.

NOODGE:

These feelings are deeply healing and are God's gift to you. Do not let anything or anyone interfere or interrupt them.

GUNNERS :

Defensive feelings. Feelings that
cause you to defend everything
you say, think and do. You've
always got your gun loaded
ready for someone to attack.

NOODGE:

Bo-o-o-rrring. Lighten up. Why would
anyone want to waste their energy
in a constant effort to shoot
you down? Are *you* always on
the attack? If so, you will
always feel defensive.
Let go. Trust more.
Hang loose.

GOTTA BEE:

Feelings that you've got to be nice, attractive, well-dressed, top dog, popular, in the crowd, on the A-list, never angered, always pleasant.

NOODGE:

Awwww come on!
Who says? If you gotta be anything,
ya gotta be *you*. And if "they"
don't like the real you, only the
pretend you, how could that make
you feel good?

YEAHBUTTS:

These are defensive feelings . . . "getting-out-of-trouble" feelings. You feel the need to defend yourself, blame someone else . . . you want 'em to know for sure that it was not your fault.

NOODGE:

The defensive Yeahbutts are about your childhood again
and stem from your fear of getting in trouble. If you are no longer
a little kid (except way down deep inside), you aren't going to
"get it." You can admit you're wrong and try to make it right.
No one is always right.

MIPS:

Feelings that make you feel like
moping. You don't even
need a reason . . .

NOODGE:

But be sure to have the Mips alone.
This is not a sharing kind of feeling.

WRANGLES:

These feelings are twisted, because what's really happening here is that you *feel* hurt — unimportant — unneeded — deserted . . . and it makes you wrangled. Wrangles happen to a lot of people used to being in control of other people's lives by virtue of controlling the purse strings (like an elderly parent who rewrites the will two or three times a year). Wrangles make you grumpy, without humor, jumpy . . . ugly to be around.

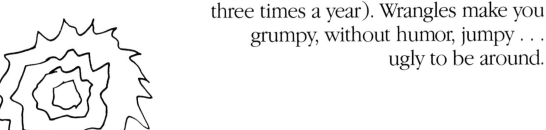

NOODGE:

Geez. No wonder. Ask yourself if you have carried the belief that you aren't worth loving except for your money. You may be pushing away the very ones you want to draw near by your sarcasm ("I haven't heard from you in so long, I'd forgotten what your voice sounds like.") You use this sarcasm to hide your hurt.

SAY, "PLEASE"...

TICKATOOS:

Feelings that make you restless . . . giggly . . . and you get Tickatoos
when you are bored with the conversation or when you get
tickled about something that no one else thinks is funny . . .
which makes you Tickatoo even harder.

NOODGE:

Nothing wrong with amusing yourself if the company is boring.
Best cure here is to find another crowd.

KAHZOOS:

Happy-go-lucky . . . the-world-is-in-my-corner feelings.

NOODGE:

Don't ask why . . .
go with the flow . . . avoid the
people who will think you're nuts or
"on something" . . . they are jealous.

SCRIPT-ITS:

Feelings of expecting a certain "script" and manner of delivery from
the person to whom you are relating. "If you would only just
say . . ." or "If you would express hurt instead of anger . . . ."
With this set of expectations, you are telling the other
person that if they don't say it the way you scripted
it and if they don't react the way you want to direct it,
it's all their fault if you aren't getting along.

NOODGE:

You are trying to get the other person to be some character you have created . . . which means that you don't want that person the way she is and you will only put up with the relationship if it follows your script. If they go along with you, you comfortably exist in only those scenes but you are keeping yourself stuck on one small stage. To step out of this, try improvisation for a while, then step into the real . . . where you can relate to all sorts of characters . . . not just those of your own making.

BIMMERS:

Feelings that are a cross between being bummed out and feeling your world has dimmed. These feelings generally point to the possibility that you are too self-absorbed.

NOODGE:

When your world is dimmed this way, it's because it takes a lot more than yourself to light up your world.

SPRINKLES:

Feelings that someone is raining on your parade . . . stealing your thunder . . . throwing cold water on your idea of fun.

NOODGE:

If you're a Sprinkler, you'll be bothered by this feeling often.
If not, why would you give a fig if another person wants
to show up as a total Neg?

WOMMBOWS:

Feelings of sudden revelation . . . as if a big rubber mallet came
down from the sky and . . . woooommmmmmbow! . . .
hit you over the head. This is related to, but even
more powerful than, the popular "aha!"

NOODGE:

How many times would you
want to be hit on the head?
Believe the revelation.

FRIKES:

Feelings of fright. Usually stemming from fear of loss . . . i.e.,
love/money/prestige/life/health.

NOODGE:

Frikes are vastly diminished when they are shared so tell someone if you can. Ask yourself what you'd feel like if the worst you feared came upon you. Then do everything you can not to allow it to happen . . . tell yourself this is a Frikening experience but will pass. It will.

PINGOS:

Feelings that keep your antennae
up, enabling you to pick up
(or mirror) whatever feelings
are going on around you.

NOODGE:

Just keep away from the Negative.

WIL-C'S:

Feelings of no commitment . . . a stall, buying time for you to
figure out a way to say no to whatever
it is you don't want to do.

NOODGE:

If you know that your answer is no, you'll save a lot of time for everyone (including yourself) if you just say so upfront. The first time you actually *say no* you'll feel weird. Practice! Practice! Practice! You'll feel wonderful when at last being upfront stops draining your energy because of worrying about it.

Feelings that you are "above it all."

NOODGE:

Oh? So, how high is up?
It's just as far down, which is
where you'll be once you fall
from your tower where the oxygen
is too thin to breathe.

BOBOS:

Feelings of hurt . . .
or feelings that your image
has been compromised.

NOODGE:

Stare at the BoBo honestly. Write it down on a piece of paper. Is it true? Does it matter? If so, let the other persons know without accusing. Listen to their answer. You might be wrong. Then throw the BoBo away in the trash.

MAY BEES:

Related to Wil-Cs . . . buying time to
save face because you know
you don't want to do
whatever it is that's
being asked of you.

TRY SAYING
"NO THANKS"...

NOODGE:

You will be kinder to the other person if you don't dish up false hope. "Letting 'em down softly" is not a kind act.

INHERITINGS:

These feelings are (hopefully) for the most part subconscious. You may have had a parent who was emotionally abusive, aloof, cold . . . wouldn't speak to you if displeased. And now, you, armed with that immense weapon of emotional pain, pull the same thing on anyone in your life whom you feel "deserves punishment," i.e., your displeasure. It gives you a feeling of control because instead of receiving pain, you are now giving pain.

NOODGE:

Do you feel good when someone you love cries because you have hurt them? And that makes you happy because it proves (to you) that they really care? Now that this has been brought out into the open (up from your subconscious), you can make yourself stop doing this. Otherwise you are enjoying your own cruelty and you'd better get some *heavy* professional help.

OWEMMES:

Feelings that "you owe me" . . . feeling
that you are not getting whatever it is
from someone you think you have paid
for in time, favors, effort or other
forms of Dewbee Investments.

NOODGE:

Do you really think that the tit-for-tat theory is operable?

GAMIES:

Feelings that cause you to believe that the person to whom you are speaking has a hidden agenda . . . is "playing a game" with you.

NOODGE:

It is said that we *all* relate to each other with a hidden agenda. Your anger at being the brunt of this "game" is there because you play games, too. It is UNfair gaming, however, if you assume without checking it out. Ask, then listen. You might have been wrong.

WUDUFS:

(Whadufs/whatifs) Feelings that worry you. ("What if I don't have enough time to figure out how I can get out of it without losing face?") Consummate procrastinators use Wudufs as a way to stay put/stagnate . . . not go forward.

NOODGE:

Ask yourself what the "if" is you are worrying about. Are you afraid you'll fail? If you never step up to the bat, you'll never strike out. But you'll never make a hit or a home run either. Do you know anyone who never, ever failed?

OHOES:

Oh-ho, you think you've got troubles, a pain, a sadness? This is a one-up feeling, demeaning and diminishing to the other person. No matter what someone else tries to tell you, you top it with an Ohoe of your own.

NOODGE:

Oh-ho on you! Someone will always come around to top you . . .
that is, if you have anyone left in your life who doesn't run
the other way when they see you coming. These
one-up Ohoes are your need to have center
stage so badly that you will even steal it.

ONE PIZZA WITH **EVERY** THING ON IT!

PIZZA

O·KEYS & DOUGH KEYS:

These are feelings that give you the control you feel good about in order to get out of feelings of being trapped (or guilty). O-Keys and Dough Keys make you feel like: "Okee-doughkee . . . I can make this choice/that option/this priority . . . ."

NOODGE:

Any choice,
option, priority, direction
will cost you something.
None of it is for free . . .
including *no* choice/
option/priority/direction.

DEW BEES:

The feeling that you "have to" or "should" do something in order to strengthen your character.

NOODGE:

Boy! They can sell a kid anything, can't they? And you're still believing it? Do you believe the sandman put that grit in your eyes?

SNUFFITS:

Feelings that make you want to snuff out the facts . . . bury them . . . ignore them . . . it never happened. Observing behavior when you were a little kid makes you absolutely certain that you want to snuff out the idea that you will soon be grown up. You may *be* a grown-up now, but secretly . . . way down deep inside, you never left your childhood.

NOODGE:

Here's the big secret no one has ever told you . . . it's good.
It's good that you have secretly put your childhood in your
pocket . . . playacting as a grown-up when the need arises
and then reaching into that secret pocket filled with your
childhood . . . to play and simply *be*.

WISTIES:

Wisties are feelings of being glad
you remembered a special
moment or victory and best of all
got to share that remembering . . .
like when you were 11 years old
and sailed your first solo race
or got to be team captain or got
the lead in the play. Wisties are
made even more wonderful
if the person to whom you are
telling all of this is genuinely
pleased along with you.

I'M SO PROUD OF YOU!

NOODGE:

Awwww. That's nice.

This is what *your* Noodge does for *you* . . . "Noodges" you along the road to be the best you can be.